Cylee

I've Been
Meaning to
Tell You

I love you !!!)

2021   *from GG*

(A book about being your friend.)

Hi.

(It's me.)

You know me so well that sometimes
I think you already know everything
I'm going to say, but just the same...

There are some things
I've been meaning to tell you.

Like, do you know how
happy you make me? Really.
This is my "thinking of you" face.

I try not to say that you're better
than everyone else, but... well...
as far as I'm concerned, you are.

It isn't just that you're fun.
Of course you're fun.

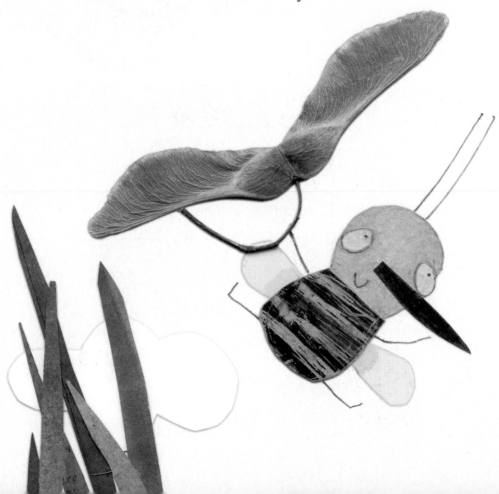

But then you're also thoughtful
and kind and sensitive and funny and
complicated and wonderful and...

You get me. You really do.

You make me feel like being myself
is more than just okay. You make me feel
like being myself is perfectly right.

(Even when that self is messy or
weird or... when my hair's uncombed
and my socks don't match.)

Sometimes, I go through pictures of us
and it lights me up just seeing our faces.
Look at us! Look at our huge smiles!

It doesn't even matter what we do.
We could wait for hours at the post office.
We could declutter my junk drawer.
We could debate about ice cream flavors
in the frozen foods aisle.

You just make things better.

How do you do it?
I don't know. It's just who you are.

So. What I've been meaning to tell you is:
Thank you. For this. This easiness.
This fun. This friendship. This us.

Because when I get to thinking about the crazy odds that, in this whole huge world, someone like you exists—someone so incredible, so brilliant, so wildly good—

And that we somehow found each other,

And got to be the best of friends...

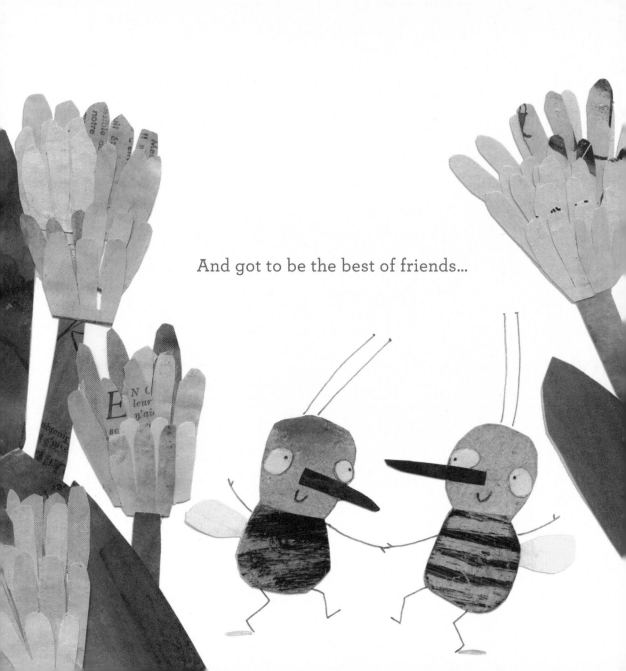

Well, it makes me pretty happy.
(Just look at me.)

COMPENDIUM.
live inspired

Written by: M.H. Clark

Edited by: Amelia Riedler

Illustrated by: Manon Gauthier

Art Directed & Designed by: Justine Edge

Library of Congress Control Number: 2017958769 | ISBN: 978-1-943200-97-9

4th printing. Printed in China with soy inks on FSC®-Mix certified paper.

Create meaningful moments with gifts that inspire.

CONNECT WITH US

live-inspired.com | sayhello@compendiuminc.com

   @compendiumliveinspired
#compendiumliveinspired